THE UNLEARNING

THE UNLEARNING

MADDY GARRETT

NEW DEGREE PRESS

THE UNLEARNING

ISBN   978-1-63676-603-4 *Paperback*

978-1-63676-262-3 *Kindle Ebook*

978-1-63676-263-0 *Ebook*

To my fellow wanderers: this book is for you. Nothing is expected of you here—just that you show up as your authentic self.

TABLE OF CONTENTS

———

AUTHOR'S NOTE

———

Letting go of a religion is completely earth-shattering yet nothing short of revolutionary. It takes a movement, an uprising of one's soul, to leave what it has always known. And like any good revolution, it does not happen all at once, and you do not win every battle. But when you come out the other side—well, the victory is sweeter than I can tell you.

When I was a young girl, I was told that my body wasn't mine to love, or give, or enjoy. I was taught that my lust was sin—as if lust was even a true concept to begin with, rather than simply a human feeling that people have tried to categorize and demonize. I carried the shame of my body and her desires with me my entire life. I wrecked romantic relationships with my holier-than-thou attitude and the shame I carried. I locked myself behind closed doors for years, hating who I was and what I desired. I hid my true self from the world and distrusted my own mind and heart.

The Christian church and its teachings made me wary of every thought I had, and I hated myself for it. "You cannot trust your mind, you cannot trust your desires," they would say. But I carried on, convincing myself that everything was okay—that these antiquated beliefs were okay. The belief that my body was a temple and I must be pure of heart and mind in order to protect her; the belief that sex was not fit for relationships outside of marriage; the belief that those who loved the same sex, or identified as a different gender, were somehow corrupted, and chose to be that way; the belief that trying to convince others of the truth I held was the main goal of life—my highest calling; the belief that I had to repent for my sins, for things that are human and natural and, quite frankly, core to my being.

I was so convinced of these ultimate truths, the infallibility of the Gospel, that I never questioned my faith. My entire reality was based on a feeling, built by several "supernatural" experiences that I labeled "God." But when those feelings continuously fluxed and flowed like everything else in my life, I couldn't help but wonder deep down if my belief in God was simply just that: a feeling.

I was caught in a battle between my beliefs and my doubts for several years, but I failed to ever truly question what I held as absolute truth. I was told at a young age to trust, not to test, God—so that's what I did. The urge to explore life on the other side of religion was always suppressed by my deep desire to be seen as competent, successful, and faithful within my Christian community and family.

It wasn't until I graduated college and left the pressure of my Christian school, friend group, and church that I began to really dig my hands into the work that had been begging me to pay attention to it my entire life. I was immersed into the secular world, had new non-religious friends and coworkers, turned 21 and went to bars, went on endless dates with boys from dating sites, and began to see parts of myself that were always repressed by my Christian way of life.

I always loved coloring inside the lines and playing by the rules, but it was difficult to keep coloring inside the lines when the lines themselves began to blur. I began to see that my body was crying out for me to accept her, weighed down by years of trying to satisfy the word of God, but all along failing to be satisfied herself; I had neglected the one thing that needed me most—my very body, my innate desires. My body had been shackled by religion long enough and she wanted to break free—*I* wanted to be free. And the universe was begging me to look at it and tell it what I saw. How did I feel when I looked up at the stars? Did it really make sense to try to put an explanation to something so vast, so inexplicable? And those labeled as outsiders by the church were calling at Christians like me to see them for who they are, *what* they are: beautiful and human.

Once the seed of uncertainty was planted, I couldn't do anything but investigate; dig; do the work; find my truth. So, I listened to dozens of podcasts on deconstruction, sexuality, and secularism. I read books with ideas about the world that were vastly different from the ones I grew up hearing. I went to bars and parties and kissed random boys and stopped "watching my mouth" and wore what I wanted to wear.

I began to see the world from a completely different perspective—so different that I could no longer deny the fact that I was living in the confines of a religious system I no longer believed in. The road was neither straight nor smooth; some days, I just wanted to revert back to the comfortable life I had been living, but I knew it was only comfortable because it was what I had always known. It was not comfortable because it was right or because it was where I belonged. I was done with being comfortable, and knew I needed to embrace this new path—a path into the unlearning.

The day I said it out loud was the day my life changed: "I am not a Christian anymore." There was nothing special about this day, but I remember being torn up by the idea of living this double life: one foot in the door of Christianity, and one foot out, crossing into the unknown of secularism and everything I'd always fought to avoid. I had no idea what was on the other side of this door, or what I would find if I decided to take a leap into the unknown. But one thing I knew for sure: if I never left this comfortable place I'd made my home in, I would never know what else the world held for me. If I kept one foot in the door of Biblical teachings and purity culture, I would never be able to fully explore or discover what else was out there—and I couldn't live with that ache, that wondering. So, I said it out loud to my reflection in the mirror. And that moment led me on the path that changed the way I see and interact with the world.

Then one night, a few months after I decided to leave the comfort of the religion I'd always known, I stepped out of the shower with a man and realized I felt not shame, but contentment for the first time in my life. That is when I knew my old self had washed away. The lies and the guilt and the distrust of my own body had vanished like the love we washed off of each other in a shower that felt like a ritual, a rebirth. But the rebirth could not have come without first facing the unlearning. The unlearning of an entire belief system, an entire life I had lived in what I thought was purity and grace but was naively wrapped in the bow of an unquestioned Christianity.

And what I found was simply *this*. The many small seconds woven into this very moment. The duality of all living things, interconnected in the simplest yet grandest of ways. This very experience, this very life; right here, right now. Bold, brilliant, beautiful, unapologetic life. The beating of hearts and the desire for bodies to keep us warm. Humanity crying out and the listeners coming to hear their stories. A universe that revolves not around us, but itself. The air trees give, the song birds sing, the life bees bring to every living thing.

I believe not that there is or isn't a god, or that the belief in a higher being is either good or bad. I simply believe everything *is*. And beyond that simple fact, not much can be said. We can tell stories and create methods for coping with life as we know it. We can lean on a god or we cannot lean on a god. If there is anything I know to be true, it is that the universe or god or whatever is out there is calling to us to go through the wilderness and see where it takes us, and stay true to who we are, no matter what others may say.

And going through the wilderness is exactly what I did. Slowly, but goddamn surely, I began to walk away from all I had ever known. I put down the books and the sermons and stopped going to church and at some point I could no longer remember the last time I had prayed or even thought about God.

This unlearning journey has taught me humans love to construct stories in order to better understand, cope with, and live in the world. We label things and then create systems in which we neatly place those things. It is human instinct to create and expand and rule over—this is apparent even in the way we have overrun this earth with our cities and towns and technologies. It is apparent in the fables of old, the ancient and new philosophies alike, that we ponder in order to feel something true and good. And most importantly this journey has taught me that in order to truly know anything, we must first go back to the basics, where we recognize that we in fact know nothing at all. Only from there, from this blank slate, can we begin to rebuild, think for ourselves, and analyze the world around us with fresh eyes. This is the only way to find yourself in a world full of people trying to be like everyone else.

Believe what you want and be who you want, but don't do it in order to fit into a certain group or mold, or to satisfy your community or parents, or to prove anything to anybody. Be you because it's the only thing you can afford to be—the only thing you can't afford to lose.

And if you don't know quite yet who you are, or what you want or what you believe—welcome. There are so many of us here on this side of the unlearning, and we can't wait to embrace you with open arms. Come, take a seat, and let me tell you a story.

You should see how the sun rises
On this side of the unlearning

It is bright and beautiful
And ceaselessly curious

PART I

GROWING UP IN IT

Spoiler Alert:
They told me that
In the beginning
God created the heavens
and the earth

But in the end
I created my own heaven
By deeply loving this earth

This earth that makes up this body
So small and fragile
Carrying me through this wonder of a world

This earth that makes up my lungs
and fills them with each breath

This earth that gives me life
And will take me back in death
Into its soil
Crisp and pungent
After a night of heavy rain

This earth
Good and gentle
Yet fierce and strong

No wonder we are made
Of the same material

Sunday morning church service
And Wednesday night youth group

Early morning worship band practice
And annual summer camp

Things that made up my adolescence
And which I remember most fondly
For giving me childhood memories
And lifelong friends

They helped me bloom into adulthood
And gave me tools to take on the world

I hold dearly these pieces
Of this religion that I loved

Sexual desire is a sin
Act on it
And you are worthy of hell

Profanity is unkind and dirty
And using the Lord's name in vain
Results in eternal punishment

Homosexuality is simply wrong
And disgusting
Sex is meant for a man and a woman
And only when married

Being drunk is disobedient
To the Word of God
And it will only bring you harm

You are worthy, loved and saved
But only if you adhere to these morals

You may be born flawed and sinful,
But He is good and will fix you
If only you trust in Him

Just have faith and He will make you clean
(But remember, if you don't follow all the rules
You will go to hell)

But He's a good, good Father!

—*The principles I was taught as an adolescent, in plain words*

When I was 5 years old
My parents walked into the living room
To see me touching myself

They were so shocked
That they laughed
Thinking it was both concerning and funny
That a five year old
Would be exploring their body
So early on

I remember feeling confused
When my parents sat me down
And told me I couldn't touch myself like that

I said I didn't know what I was doing
It just felt good

They told me that it was bad
And that I couldn't do it again

And from that moment on
I believed my body
And its pleasure
Was something to be avoided
At all costs

In church small groups I always felt like
The rotten one in the bunch
The one with bad desires
And reckless behavior

Like secretly watching porn
And exploring my sexuality
Slowly but surely
With both boys
And myself

I bottled up the frustration and shame
And said to myself
What I thought my church friends would say to me
If they found out how dirty I was

You're disgusting
You're impure
You don't deserve a love like Jesus'
Because you can't stop touching your body
The way only your husband should one day

I never talked about how I was feeling
Or the things I was thinking and doing
Because I never felt safe
Telling my deepest fears and desires
To people I thought would judge me
For being less pure than they were

This competition
To be seen as the holiest Christian
While suppressing my desires

Led to an unspoken depression
That buried me alive
In the hole my shame had carved
Within me

Like any Christian
My faith came and went in waves

Fervent one week
And scrambling for any ounce of God the next

There would be weeks
Where I couldn't stop listening to worship music
And I couldn't put my Bible down
Day after day I would crave the feeling of
Immersing myself in the Lord

And then other weeks
A drought would come after the rain
I would forget to pray
Avoid picking up my daily devotional
And question my place and purpose in the world

Faith, like life itself,
is a roller coaster

I had highs and lows and in-betweens
But I held on tight to God no matter what

And I never, ever doubted
That I was here for a reason

Looking back
I can see how this tumultuous relationship
With a God I could only sometimes feel
Was setting the stage for a life
Filled with uncertainty, trauma bonds
And an addiction to chaos

I thought life was supposed to be so up and down
All the time
I was told that having your faith come and go
Was normal

But how can you be okay with an idea of normal
That leaves you feeling confused and empty
More than half of your life?

I always felt like there were so many contradictions
Within the Christian doctrine

Like God's loving nature
Yet his ability to massacre thousands
Without even flinching

Or the calling to love everyone
And care for the poor,
To give up one's earthly possessions
And put worth in helping others

Yet I saw wealthy, white families
Volunteering to feed the homeless
Only on holidays
And thinking that was enough serving
To get them by until next year

—*This is what being a good Christian looks like*

In elementary school
My next door neighbor was my best friend

She and her family were not Christian
And I remember this constantly plaguing my mind
Wondering if I was ever going to save their souls

We did most things together
Including weekend sleepovers

I hated having sleepovers on Saturday nights
Because I felt embarrassed
To ask her to church with my family and I
On Sunday morning

I think even at such an early age
I knew there was something inherently wrong
About trying to convince another human
A friend
That your way of seeing life
Is better than theirs

I simultaneously felt
Both despair
That her soul was lost
Thinking my childhood best friend
Would burn in hell
And shame
For having those thoughts
About someone I loved

How could someone so innocent
Be subject to hell
Simply because she was not raised
The same way I was?

It all felt wrong
So early on

I once told a boy whom I loved
That the only way I would
Feel that I lived a purposeful life
Is if I surrendered to God's plan

I believed wholeheartedly
That my greatest purpose
Was to save as many people as possible
For Jesus

Whatever path in life
Led me to impact the most people
And lead the most people to God,
That was the only life I wanted to live

I was willing to sacrifice anything
In my life
If it meant saving even just one more soul
For the Kingdom

The boy told me
That he didn't know
If he could ever make that commitment

He told me I had a bigger heart than him
If I was willing to give up anything
Just to save one more soul

It made me feel like the ultimate Christian
To say I would lay down everything
In Jesus' name

But I can't help but wonder
How I would have felt if I actually had to

—*I wonder what he thinks of me now*

I grew up so engulfed by Christianity
That it felt like the core piece of my being

It was never even a question in my mind
Of whether or not I would attend
A Christian university
I didn't feel I would fit in
With the partying, sex and drugs
Of state schools and Ivy Leagues

Every life decision I made
Hinged upon the question
Of whether or not God was calling me
In that direction

I would pray intently
And try to discern the voice of God
So that he was the sole decision-maker
In my life

So I attended a Christian school
And sang in chapel
And led Bible studies
And did morning devotionals

My life was so centered around God
That the idea of there not being one
Never had the time to cross my mind

To my parents:
I know you pushed a faith on me
Because you loved me too much not to

You taught me about the one thing
That your life depends on
The one thing that stops the aching in your bones
And the longing of your soul

No wonder you wanted to show me the love of Jesus
When it has saved you from your darkest times
And led you into some of your best

I know you love me deeply
And for that, I thank you

I thank you for doing
Whatever you thought it was
That would give me the most
Out of this life

I thank you for teaching me
Everything you knew and loved

Although we no longer
See eye to eye
About the religion you raised me in,

And even though I have chosen to rebuild somewhere else
You are still my foundation
And you always will be

My childhood was ultimately marked by shame
For never feeling good enough

And also an
Eternal
Internal
Ache

An ache for an existence that
Didn't depend on
Needing to repent
Any and every time
I had a bad thought or
Stepped out of line
According to some Biblical teachings

My childhood hardly felt like a childhood at all

How can it, when you are constantly aware
Of your missteps, shortcomings and flaws?

How can it, when you are constantly trying
To just be good enough to be saved?

How can it, when the God you love
More than anything in this world
Can decide to either save you
Or send you to an eternal hell?

Tell me
How can you have a real childhood
When you are living in a nightmare
You cannot escape?

PART II

THE
QUESTIONING

The beginning of the unlearning
Is the most unsettling
Igniting a fire in your bones
Unaccustomed to the heat of the flames

Caught between two worlds
One you've always known and trusted
And one you've been told not to trust
But are dying to know

Endlessly curious about the world you can see
Just in view
But that feels out of reach
Yet indebted to the one you are in

The church taught me
That the human mind was weak
And it could never understand every
Teaching or event
From the Bible

I was told by the leaders
To trust in God
Because one day all the pain
And confusion of the world
Would make perfect sense

But if the human mind is so fallible
How can we claim to know that
There even is one truth, one God?

If we are to distrust our own mind so much
How can we justify
Entering neighborhoods and countries
That are not our own
Trying to convince them what we believe to be real?
How can we know any of this *is* real?

—*I have so many questions*

The way that my soul drifts
From needing validation
Needing to be seen as amicable
Obedient, good
By my Christian community

To feeling so much rage and confusion
And angst to get out of this tight skin
That religion put me in

Feels like having a conversation
About politics
With someone you love and respect
But very much disagree with

You want to be seen as competent,
Understanding, tolerant and learned
While all the while feeling the passion
Of the debate boil your skin
So that everything becomes numb

I have grown numb to the pain of staying
As well as the longing to leave

The numbness has become
A complacency
That I do not know how to shake
But that I know I need to

I know the trajectory of my life
Depends on it.

—*You can only live as your truest self when you confront*
the numbness

I have never made a home of this body
For the keys have never belonged to me

The church told me my body was of this earth
And only served me harm in this life
But if I just held on for a little while,
I would be rid of it and all sinful desires
Once I ascended to heaven

I want to rip the skin off of my forearms
And discover the pulse that lies beneath it

I want to undress and feel vulnerable
Until I cannot hide anything
Not the scar on my stomach
Or the tips of my breasts
Or the desires that I've felt my entire life in this body

I am beginning to strip down all of the insecurities
That have been shoved down my throat
And have seeped into my bloodstream

I am beginning to take off this skin
And drain this blood
After years of aching
Years of yearning

I will continue to question
Continue to dig deeper
Continue to unravel
Until I am merely bones

And maybe then
I can finally rebuild
A body that feels like home

When I was nineteen years old
I dated a boy from my church

I had confidence that he was a man of God
And a believer in His word

But the thoughts and ideas he held
About God and Biblical doctrine
Had me questioning everything I knew

How could this boy not believe in sin?
How can a Christian think that
So many of the stories in the Bible
Are simply metaphors?
What do you mean God isn't
The image of a man, a father?
You think God could be a woman?

There were so many questions
I had failed to explore
And they were suddenly spiraling
In my mind and destroying
So many of the foundations
I thought were solid as rock
But that were torn up by the simplest of questions

I began listening to every podcast
And reading every book
I could get my hands on
Trying to figure out if this religion
I had based my entire life on
Was a delusion or not

But I found the answers
Buried much deeper than the research
In the very foundations I had built
For myself as an adolescent

In order to find those answers
And know if I really believed this story
I had been told my entire life

I had to go to the source
Rip up the foundations
Put shovel to hard ground
Dig away all I had known
And rebuild from the rubble

It is only when we deconstruct
A narrative
That we can begin to fully understand it
And then choose to either accept it as truth
Or find it at fault
And reject it altogether

The thing about your inner voice
Is that it will never go away

The longer you ignore it
The louder it gets

So when you hear that voice
Please
listen

Instead of running away
Lean in

Maybe
It is a part of the human condition
To abandon the things
Closest to us
Like a lioness leaving her cubs
So that she may carry on
Find another mate
Create more life

And so that the cubs may grow
To be as strong and independent
As their mother proved herself to be

They will learn so much
In the wilderness of the unknown

And this can only happen if they
Abandon their dependent selves entirely
Lifting the brush to the canvas
Of their unlearning, their becoming

Maybe
It is more than just a human condition
To abandon the things
Closest to us

Maybe
That is how all living things grow

I have too much kindle and spark
And raging fire within me
To be confined to some narrow set
Of rules and standards

I was born to burn them out
Of this home

This home that
Carries far too much woman
For your straw narrative

One strike of a match
And all of your labels and lies
Go up in flames

I used to wish
The rain would come
And wash you off of me

But I realized
Rain can't wash away
Something that has taken root
Inside your soul

—*I'll need a hurricane*

I loved you with all of my being
But like most love stories
I knew it was time to let you go

PART III

THE LETTING GO

Unlearning an entire system is difficult
When you have no new, packaged one to learn

Rather than switching one for another
You slowly inspect each aspect of the current system
And continuously trade out old, rusty parts
For new ones
Evaluating what is helpful and good
And what is no longer useful nor productive

This happens piece by piece
Slowly forming a new system
That no longer fits into any mold

Falling out of love with God
And the community I had built around Him
Was like breaking up with a longtime boyfriend

It is nearly inexplicable
Why I had fallen out of love after so long
But it was clear that I had

No longer felt the excitement
Of talking to that person after a long day

Dates felt more like something I had to
Fit into my busy schedule
Than something I made time for

And avoiding the topic
When friends ask how we are doing

Because I didn't really know
Or I did
And I just didn't want to admit it

The falling out of love is not swift or ill-meaning
It is simply a feeling
Of distance, of drifting, of moving on

It is true
When they say
"When you know, you know"

I don't want your house in the suburbs
And Wednesday night small groups
And two kids with a baby on the way

I don't want your stability
Or certainty in the world or your God
I don't want to pretend like I am fully known
By some God I cannot see

I want to be scattered and reckless
And wild and also
Whole
And totally myself
Totally *free*

—*Things I never admitted but always felt*

Why is it
That the warmth of a stranger's bed
And his body pressed against mine
Feels more like home
Than the world I had built
Inside of this religion?

If there is a hell
I have already lived through it

If there is a hell
It is questioning your own body
Fearing your own deepest desires

If there is a hell
It is feeling as though
You will never live up to the expectations
Of everyone you love
Because you do not desire the
Neat Christian life
Of church on Sundays
A nice husband
And obedient children

If there is a hell
It is in the notion that
You and your desires alone
Will never be good enough
Or pure enough
Or whole enough
Unless you let a God
Decide for you what is good
And what is not
That you are good
Or not

If your God
Can strike down
An entire nation of people
Without flinching
And calling in justice
I don't want Him

If your God doesn't think that
Love is love is love is love
I don't want Him

If your God
Can murder his own son
And call it the moment
We were all saved from our filth
I don't want Him

If your God
Can send someone to hell
Simply for not being able to
Understand or grasp
The universe and His existence
I don't want Him

How do you put into words
A divorce from a lover
That left you picking shards of yourself
Off the floor
Attempting to coax them back together
While trying to avoid stepping
On their sharp edges

How do you tell someone
About a love ending
When you are not sure
If it was really ever love at all?

My mother suggested that maybe
My life after the unlearning
Didn't feel different
Because I did not ever really know
The love of God

But if that is true
And I poured twenty-one years of my life into a God
That I still couldn't grasp or feel

Then I do not want a part of that religion
At all

When I let go
Of the one thing
I ever fully committed to

It felt as if I had
Failed
As if my world had
Shattered

But perhaps commitment
Isn't the great goal after all

Maybe there is power
In not belonging to anything
Except yourself

I left because you were toxic
Not because I didn't try hard enough
I tried
With fervent prayer
With seeking visions
With daily Bible readings
With small groups and accountability partners
With boundless love and grace and hope in my heart

I tried
With every ounce of my being
For twenty-one years
And never found what I was looking for

That is the definition of insanity
Doing the same thing
Over and over again
Expecting different results

Just as the leaves cheer
As the wind blows wildly by

So the universe rejoices
When you move
And shift
And change

—*Nothing in nature is meant to be stagnant*

For once in my life
My growth isn't centered around
Purifying every inch of myself
Until I'm sparkling like church glass

It is now about digging my hands in the dirt
Finding out what it means to struggle
Lunging into the fire
Instead of fleeing from the flames

It is about rolling around in the mud
Discovering everything the earth has to offer
Simply finding myself dirty
And feeling no need to cleanse

I have always been one
To thrive off of certainty—
Knowing right from wrong
Having all the facts

But I am learning
That there is beautiful growth
And unexpected peace
In accepting life and the universe
For the vast, unknown
Anomaly that it is

It is here
In the uncertainty,
Where I don't know my way,
That I know I must not turn back

PART IV

THE REBIRTH

My heart knew I was not where I should be
Long before the unlearning

It was my mind
And my ego
That needed to be convinced

When I let go of my old perception of God
I let go of my old perception of self

I no longer see myself as broken, sinful, or in need of saving

I see myself—my body, mind and soul—
As the perfect trinity
A source of goodness and beauty

All that I need is, and always has been,
Within me

I used to look at the world around me
And see an explanation

I saw do's and don'ts
Shoulds and Shouldn'ts

I saw a capital-T Truth
That explained everything that mattered
And that I trusted when things couldn't be explained

Now I see questions,
Far too many to think there could ever be
A simple explanation

I see now that believing there is an underlying answer
To everything in the universe
Is not Truth
But trust

I watched the universe expand
Into millions of pieces
Before my eyes

It became larger and more complex
And far more interesting
Once I stepped away from my religion

I am not yet sure
How to put all of the pieces
Back together
But I know the bigger picture
Will never look the same

Like an orchid growing bigger every day
There comes a point where you must re-pot
And you cannot again fit it into the
One it began in

—Things that grow will always require more room

Walking among the pines
Needles crunching under my boots
I take a deep breath
I inhale the universe
All of existence fills my lungs
And I feel the culmination of all the
Peace and purpose that has ever been

Lying on the night-painted earth
My eyes wrap around the stars
Like a warm, familiar blanket
I feel the expanse of creation
It shrinks
And I hold it in my stillness

Standing in a field
The warm sun climbs down from its pedestal
Enveloping me
And all of the love that has
Reverberated throughout history
Sinks into my skin
A sweet, warm embrace

Sometimes I graze my fingertips
Over long blades of grass

Just so I can feel the vitality
Of the Universe
Pulse through my hands

It feels like energy
Running through my body

The energy that has run through every living thing
Runs, too, through me

Sometimes I cradle the face of a flower
Still attached to its roots

Just to relearn that there are living things
That have also experienced so many seasons
So many growing pains
So many transformations
And nevertheless they bloom

Beautifully,
They bloom

Long drives through the mountains at dusk
Mornings spent journaling at my desk
Damp forests after a cool, spring rain
Intimate moments with my own two hands
Potting soil and gardening gloves
Starry skies in the middle of the desert

My mind,
A refuge
My body,
A home

—*My new places of worship*

I once loved a boy
Because I thought he was holy

I let him give me a diamond ring
Because he told me I was his only

When I began to see he had more flaws
Than I originally knew

I took it as my Christian obligation
To fix him and make him new

What I learned is that you can't change people
No matter how hard you try

And thinking that you can
Is just a Christian lie

I have torn myself ruthless
Over the mistakes I made

And although my love for him stands
The guilt and shame have not stayed

When that love one day ended
Half of my heart went with it too

But for my heartbreak and mistakes
I now see the blame is on You.

You told me the world was cold and painful
That sin would cause me more hurt
Than good
But on this side of things
I have found that
The thing that has hurt me most in life
Is the limiting belief
That I am constrained
To act a certain way
Believe a certain way
Love a certain way
Be a certain way

I stepped into the shower with a man
And we washed our love off of each other

I stepped out of the shower
And realized it was the first time
I had not felt shame after being intimate

That's when I knew
I had washed this religion off of me too

I used to see my body as a temple
Never to be touched or explored

Now I see her as a vast landscape
With so many
Beautiful places to traverse

A treasure hunt
Where the chest
Is only the beginning

—*You must dig to find the gold*

It feels like a gift
To no longer base my worth
Off of some god's measurements

Oh how good it feels
To be secure and worthy
Fully and simply by being me

—*This is freedom*

I am not broken
And I never was

People were right to call me sheltered
As a young, Christian girl

I lived in my shelter
My shielded place of protection
For twenty-one years
Before realizing that I am
Most found, most whole
Most free, most secure
In the wilderness

What I thought I was being
Protected from this entire time
This freedom
Has ended up being the very thing
That brings me life

Once I left
I understood that I had been in chains
The entire time

I want to do something
That scares the shit out of me

I want to bike down the steepest mountainside
And backpack alone through the wilderness
And bungee jump off the tallest building

And I want to fall in love with myself
Over
And over
And over again

If we are what the church calls
The lost generation

I am happy to be a part of it

Happy to love myself and my peers
For who we are
And not what we are told to be

We are young and rebellious, maybe
But free and right where we belong

I have learned that
You can hold something with certainty
While also realizing you may be
Certainly wrong

Like loving somebody with all of your being
Even though you know
They may not actually be "the one"

Yet you know with certainty
That you still love them all the same

I think this is the only wise way
To hold something at all

For thinking you know anything without a doubt
Would be awfully limiting
Considering the possibilities that lie
Deep within these grounds
Waiting to be explored and seen

For those who hold with certainty
That an acorn is just an acorn
Will never know the monstrous tree
That can grow if it is
Planted, watered, transformed

If life is a symphony
I have just drawn the curtains open

I have just stepped into the light
Refusing to let anything
But the rhythm of my courage
Lead me through the performance of a lifetime

Maybe this is what I have been preparing for
This entire time
This is my moment to shine
This is my moment
This
Is the stage I have been looking for

PART V

WHAT I WOULD GO BACK AND TELL MYSELF

The unlearning
Is too vast to occur quickly or smoothly
But too important to stop from happening

It takes on many forms
Rejecting any sense
Of knowable shape or timeline
Salient and unshakable
It drowns out the possibility of returning
To a state of unconscious bliss

I have only the bliss that is now
And that is ahead
The true, knowing bliss that comes with
The unlearning

Our bodies are not meant to be stagnant

Neither are our minds
And hearts
And beliefs

Every living thing is meant to stretch
And ache and feel
And grow

You do not exist
To sit idly by
While you let others tell you
How to live your own goddamn life

You were made to embrace all that is happening
Even when things might feel awkward
Or uncomfortable or terrifying

You are on this earth to go through
All of this change and growth
To experience pain and joy and everything in between

You exist
To rise to the occasion
To rise from the ashes
Of the lies and hardships you leave behind

And I promise you, dear one
That you can, and will, leave them behind

So hold on tight, because this all means something
Even if you can't see the bigger picture yet

You have so much life ahead of you
And I cannot wait for you to
Live this life
Your life

The way you want to
The way you were always meant to
Which is your home

Failing to examine your comfortability
Is the biggest hindrance
To growth

Never looking at the life you've created
From the outside
Or unraveling what you have always known and believed
Is how we breed ignorance and stagnation

And when we are stagnant we cannot grow
We cannot live to our fullest potential

So when you feel that maybe you don't belong
In this place you've settled down in
When you feel the urge
To peel back the layers
And discover something new

Please,
listen;
Please,
question;
Please,
grow

Even the plants can't help growing
Toward the light

You, too, will find your sun
And you will bud
In the direction
Of beautiful, undeniable light

Just like a tree
You are only as tall
As strong
As beautiful
As your roots are deep

You must do the work
The hard, inner work
That no one can see

Otherwise you will never grow
To your fullest potential
Your fullest beauty

—*Show me what a sequoia looks like*

To my body:

I am sorry the church demonized you
I am sorry I thought you were bad

It is an absolute shame
That I have neglected your desires
For my entire life

But it is so nice to meet you here
On this side of the unlearning

What a joy to know that you are good
And that I can enjoy every inch of you

And that it is my right
And my decision alone
To let whomever I want
Enjoy you too

Your own body is as bright
And beautiful
As the stars you gaze up at

It is as strong
As the redwoods
Standing tall
Whether their leaves are budding
Or falling

It is as resilient
As a diamond
Under the heat and pressure
Of the world

Your body is with you
Through all of your struggles
In this life

Start treating it like the
Glorious, magnificent
Survivor that it is

Looking at the universe around you
With awe and wonder
Is the most important thing you can do

For when you truly understand
That each object in this universe
Is an individual miracle and masterpiece

You begin to truly know and feel
That same awe and wonder for yourself
For your own body, your own soul

I know that you are feeling lost
And you are scared of the path that lies ahead
Because it will come with so much difficulty

But I am here to tell you that it is going to be more than okay
It is going to be hard many days
But at the end of it all
There will be magic

Because you are magic
And all that you seek is worth the exploration
If you know in your heart
There is something more calling your name

There is something more calling your name
Go out, seek it
And you will find more than you could have ever imagined

Coffee may keep you going for the day
And sex may please you in the moment

Vacations may satisfy you for a week
And alcohol may feel good for the night

And your idea of a God might make
Your longing soul feel more at ease

But honey,
The only thing that can save you
Is you

When you are living within
A belief system and its community
But you want to escape this heaviness
You have called home

It can often feel impossible
To find a listening ear
Someone who understands

I often did not feel lonely
In my questioning
Because I had found a community
In podcasts, books, articles, social media

It is amazing how shared experiences
Between even strangers
Can heal loneliness
In such a difficult time

—*Find your strangers*

You are so brave
For taking on this task of finding yourself
And figuring out what life means for you

What a huge task for one human
And yet here you are
Taking it on one breath at a time

Breathe in, dear one
There is so much to see!
Breathe out, my love
There is so much yet to unlearn

It is difficult work, yes
But the work you were meant for
And it is done only by those strong as you
Dedicated as you, real and raw and true as you

—*You were meant for this*

Like forests need a fire
Every few decades
To regenerate life
And make it flourish even fuller

So we must burn
Our systems
Our beliefs
Our ways of doing things
So that we can
Begin to flourish again too

It will get easier
As you begin to see what is waiting for you
On the other side

Growing up means
Realizing your parents aren't perfect

That they have flaws and hardships
And things you cannot see

But all the while
They cherished you
Protected you
Loved you
Fought for you
Even when you couldn't see it

Growing up means
Realizing there is much more to life
And to other human beings
Than what you can see

And that is okay
For without growth, the colors of spring
Would not be as beautiful

When you look at the world with brand new eyes

You are bound to see
Beautiful, brand new things

When I decided to drop the veil of my religion
And see the world through fresh, unbiased eyes
I began to see things I never saw before:

The beauty in another person's nakedness
The vulnerability of intimacy

The beauty of sleepless nights
Spent dancing and drinking with friends

The beauty of seeing the universe
Not as one limited path or story
But as millions of stories and experiences
And truths
Awaiting you to see all of its possibilities

You cannot live
An extraordinary life
When you are stuck
In the ordinary stories
You grew up with

Honey, it is time to grow
Time to go off on your own journey
Time to heal from past wounds
And find new and beautiful paths

There is an extraordinary story
That is waiting to be found
Right in front of you

The journey through the unlearning
Has been neither easy nor smooth

But it has been nothing short of
A revolution

And the fun has just begun
Because now the real adventure begins

The adventure that lay
On this side of the unlearning

ACKNOWLEDGMENTS

To my dear friends: thank you for finding me and loving me and letting me find and love myself. Thank you for sticking by my side through the beautiful and the broken. And thank you for lifting me up, always.

To my publisher, editors, and everyone involved at the Creators Institute: You are the reason this book is in the hands of its reader right now. None of this would have been possible without you. I am honored and grateful and every cliche word you've begged me not to use.

To friends, family, acquaintances, and others who made this dream a reality by pre-ordering a copy of my book: The faith you put in me and this book means more than I could ever try to tell you. Thank you to:

Alyse Hausman
Alyssa Paylor
Analise Nelson
Andre Jones
Andrea Grohovsky
Andrew Yost
Anna Blaszkiw
Arden O. Martinez
Arielle Taramasco
Ashley Guzik

Bailey Rowan
Blaine Tiongson
Brandi Steele
Brett Filippin
Brett Noble
Brittney Siordia
Bryan McFarland
Carly Steinberg
Charles Burkland
Charlotte Hembree

Bailee Noella

Daria Szepkouski

David Gladson

Don Garrett

Donna Garrett

Donna Garrett

Dylan Gurga

Eliza Jason

Elizabeth Sampson

Emily Rojas

Emma DeBorde

Eric Koester

Erin Mulligan

German Duarte

Haley Lesser

Jacqueline Parker

Javier Cifuentes-Garzaro

Jen Miramontes

Jenna Luallen

Jessica Hall

Jon Hoskins

Jonah McStay

Jordan Goodman

Jordan Lee

Joshua Lee Burke

Julia Weidman

Justin Lewis

Justin Stokes

Kaitlyn Bergstrom

Chelsea Hefti

Katherine Castigliola

Khaula Mahmood

Kristen Ledesma

Kristina Simmons

Kylie Garrett

Lauren Carlson

Lauren Cazares

Lauren Detreville

Lex Yardley

Lindsay Whiteman

Lindsey Lupo

Lisa Scott

Lizzy Kim

Lori Gilmore

Lori Stokes

Madie Thomas

Madison Elick

Mark Bankert

Marlee Beauchamp

Martha Basurto

Mary Walden

McKenna Bell

Megan Acree

Megan Scheuber

Meghan Basurto

Melanie Fountain

Mike Kaich

Natasha Johnson

Kassidy Averill
Pamela Nguyen
Peyton Rose
Rachael Kelch
Rachel Best
Rachel Preleyko
Rachel Sawyer
Rebecca Salgado

Nina Galvan
Ricard C. Smith, Ed.
Scott Logan
Sue Golubics
Taeshon Greene
Tanner Ralls
Tara Campbell
Yvonne Covarrubias